FUN WITH MATH
Measuring

A Crabtree Roots Book

DOUGLAS BENDER

CRABTREE
Publishing Company
www.crabtreebooks.com

School-to-Home Support for Caregivers and Teachers

This book helps children grow by letting them practice reading. Here are a few guiding questions to help the reader with building his or her comprehension skills. Possible answers appear here in red.

Before Reading:

- What do I think this book is about?
  - *I think this book is about measuring and numbers.*
  - *I think this book teaches us different ways to measure things.*
- What do I want to learn about this topic?
  - *I want to learn what tools I can use to measure things.*
  - *I want to learn about different kinds of measurements.*

During Reading:

- I wonder why...
  - *I wonder why people use numbers in measuring.*
  - *I wonder why people measure how heavy things are.*
- What have I learned so far?
  - *I have learned that a ruler measures length.*
  - *I have learned that people use measurements all the time.*

After Reading:

- What details did I learn about this topic?
  - *I have learned that there are different tools used for measuring.*
  - *I have learned that measurements tell us how long or heavy things are.*
- Read the book again and look for the vocabulary words.
  - *I see the word **ruler** on page 7 and the word **scale** on page 10. The other vocabulary words are found on page 14.*

We use numbers in **measuring**.

These **books** are big!

A **ruler** can help us find out how long they are.

We can also find out how **heavy** they are!

We can use a **scale.**

11

People use **measurements** all the time!

Word List

Sight Words

a	help	these
all	how	they
are	in	time
big	long	us
can	out	use
find	the	we

Words to Know

books

heavy

measurements

measuring

ruler

scale

40 Words

We use numbers in **measuring**.

These **books** are big!

A **ruler** can help us find out how long they are.

We can also find out how **heavy** they are!

We can use a **scale**.

People use **measurements** all the time!

Written by: Douglas Bender

Designed by: Rhea Wallace

Series Development: James Earley

Proofreader: Janine Deschenes

Educational Consultant: Marie Lemke M.Ed.

Photographs:
Shutterstock: Karen roach: cover; Chulleporn:
    cover; Bragin Alexey: cover; Swettie Rice: p. 3,
    14; Kokhanchikov: p. 5, 6, 9, 14; New Africa: 11, 14;
    Dragon Images: p. 13, 14

Library and Archives Canada Cataloguing in Publication

Title: Measuring / Douglas Bender.
Names: Bender, Douglas, 1992- author.
Description: Series statement: Fun with math |
    "A Crabtree roots book".
Identifiers: Canadiana (print) 2021019572X |
    Canadiana (ebook) 20210195738 |
    ISBN 9781427156280 (hardcover) |
    ISBN 9781427156341 (softcover) |
    ISBN 9781427133519 (HTML) |
    ISBN 9781427134110 (EPUB) |
    ISBN 9781427156525 (read-along ebook)
Subjects: LCSH: Measurement—Juvenile literature.
Classification: LCC QA465 .B46 2022 | DDC j530.8—dc23

Library of Congress Cataloging-in-Publication Data

CIP available at Library of Congress

Crabtree Publishing Company

www.crabtreebooks.com   1-800-387-7650

Copyright © 2022 **CRABTREE PUBLISHING COMPANY**   Printed in the U.S.A./062021/CG20210401

Published in the United States
Crabtree Publishing
347 Fifth Avenue, Suite 1402-145
New York, NY, 10016

Published in Canada
Crabtree Publishing
616 Welland Ave.
St. Catharines, Ontario L2M 5V6